UPDOG

IN THE SPOTLIGHT

DUA LIPA

POP AND FASHION ICON

Heather E. Schwartz

Lerner Publications ◆ Minneapolis

Lerner Publications Company
An imprint of Lerner Publishing Group, Inc.
241 First Avenue North
Minneapolis, MN 55401 USA

For reading levels and more information, look up this title at www.lernerbooks.com.

Main body text set in ITC Franklin Gothic Std.
Typeface provided by Adobe Systems.

Editor: Angel Kidd **Photo Editor:** Angel Kidd

Library of Congress Cataloging-in-Publication Data

Names: Schwartz, Heather E., author.
Title: Dua Lipa : pop and fashion icon / Heather E. Schwartz.
Description: Minneapolis : Lerner Publications, 2025. | Series: In the spotlight (Updog books) | Includes bibliographical references and index. | Audience: Ages 8–11 | Audience: Grades 2–3 | Summary: "Dua Lipa won Best New Artist at the 2019 Grammy awards and has had fantastic success ever since. Fans around the world are mesmerized by her catchy beats and will love reading about her life!"— Provided by publisher.
Identifiers: LCCN 2024037256 (print) | LCCN 2024037257 (ebook) | ISBN 9798765669198 (library binding) | ISBN 9798765684504 (paperback) | ISBN 9798765679135 (epub)
Subjects: LCSH: Lipa, Dua, 1995-—Juvenile literature. | Singers—Biography—Juvenile literature.
Classification: LCC ML3930.L563 S38 2025 (print) | LCC ML3930.L563 (ebook) | DDC 782.42164092 [B]—dc23/20230223

LC record available at https://lccn.loc.gov/2024037256
LC ebook record available at https://lccn.loc.gov/2024037257

Manufactured in the United States of America
1-1011539-53890-10/23/2024

TABLE OF CONTENTS

Strong Singer

Dua Lipa grinned when she won her third Grammy award in 2021!

Dua's family is from the country Kosovo. She was born in London.

As a child, she liked singing. A teacher told her she was not a good singer.

Dua then went to a theater school. She learned she had talent after all.

As a teenager, Dua was a restaurant server and model in London.

But she wanted to be a singer.

She put songs on YouTube and made demos.

In 2014, she got a record deal. She released her first single, "New Love," in 2015.

UP NEXT!

Making music.

World Famous

In 2016, Lipa started a charity to help people in Kosovo.

She released her debut album in 2017. It had three hit songs.

Her songs made her famous around the world.

In 2018, Lipa and her father started a music festival in Kosovo.

STAR STATS

Full name: Dua Lipa

Date of birth: August 22, 1995

Hometown: London, UK

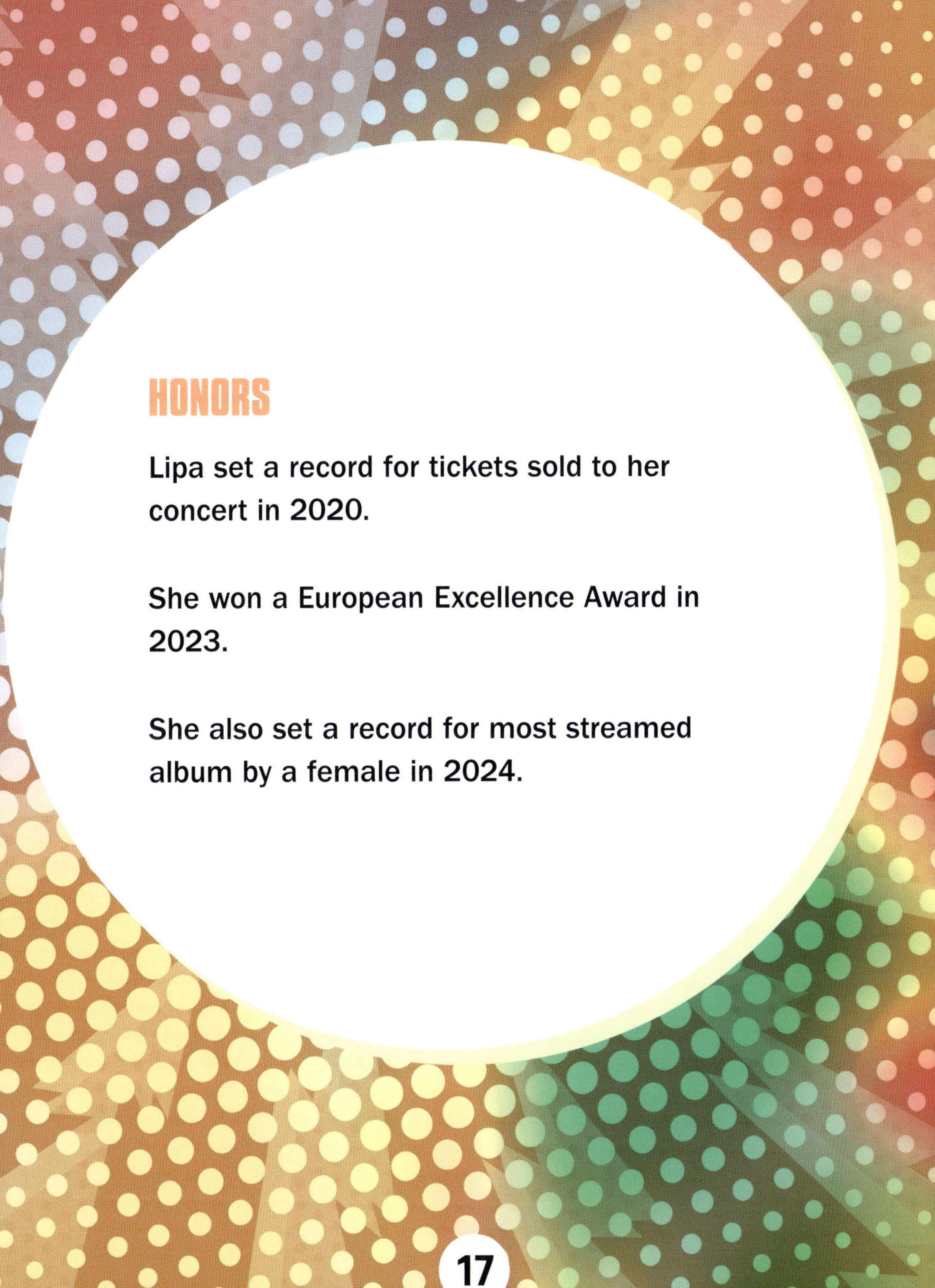

HONORS

Lipa set a record for tickets sold to her concert in 2020.

She won a European Excellence Award in 2023.

She also set a record for most streamed album by a female in 2024.

In 2019, Lipa won two Grammys.

She put out her second album, *Future Nostalgia*, in 2020.

That year, she played a concert on a live stream. Millions watched.

She won Best Pop Vocal Album at the Grammys in 2021.

UP NEXT!

Getting personal.

More Than Music

In 2022, Lipa started the newsletter Service95. It's also a website, podcast, and book club.

She writes and talks about her interests, such as reading and fashion.

In 2023, she was in the movie *Barbie*.

Lipa also helped design a clothing line that year.

She spoke up on how she felt about world events.

Her third album
came out in 2024.

Lipa is excited for her future. She will work on her music and much more.

Just like Dua Lipa

Lipa practiced to become a great singer. What is a skill you can practice to become better at it? What could you do with the skill?

GLOSSARY

charity: a group that gives help and money to people in need

debut: first

demo: music made to show a performer's abilities

live stream: an event shown live over the internet

newsletter: a collection of articles about particular interests or events

talent: natural skill or ability

CHECK IT OUT!

Britannica Kids: Kosovo
https://kids.britannica.com/kids/article/Kosovo/346157

Fun Kids: Top 10 Facts About Dua Lipa!
https://www.funkidslive.com/learn/top-10-facts/top-10-facts-about-dua-lipa/

Kiddle: Dua Lipa Facts for Kids
https://kids.kiddle.co/Dua_Lipa

Martin, Steve, *I Like the Performing Arts . . . What Jobs Are There?* Tulsa: Kane Miller, 2022.

Rains, Dalton. *Pop Music*. Mendota Heights, MN: Focus Readers, 2025.

Rose, Rachel. *Ariana Grande: Pop Vocal Powerhouse*. Minneapolis: Lerner Publications, 2026.

INDEX

PHOTO ACKNOWLEDGMENTS

Image credits: Kevin Winter/Getty Images, pp. 4, 21; ARMEND NIMANI/Getty Images, pp. 5, 12, 15; Kirstin Sinclair/Getty Images, pp. 6, 8; Yui Mok - PA Images/Getty Images, p. 7; Manfred Schmid/Getty Images, p. 9; Roger Kisby/Getty Images, p. 10; Matt Winkelmeyer/Getty Images, p. 11; Timothy Hiatt/Getty Images, p. 13; John Phillips/Getty Images, p. 14; AP Photo/Rob Grabowski/Invision, p. 16; Alberto E. Rodriguez/Getty Images, p. 18; Gareth Cattermole/Getty Images, p. 19; 2020 Pandora Media LLC/Getty Images, p. 20; MediaPunch/Bauer-Griffin/Getty Images, p. 22; Christopher Polk/Getty Images, p. 23; Anadolu/Getty Images, p. 24; Emma McIntyre/Getty Images, p. 25; Kevin Mazur/Getty Images, p. 26; AP Photo/Joel C Ryan/Invision, p. 27; AP Photo/zz/KGC-03/STAR MAX/IPx, p. 28. Design elements: oxygen/Getty Images; Medesulda/Getty Images.

Cover image: AP Photo/Rob Grabowski/Invision.